Philanthropy as Amplifier

How Catalytic Capital Can Transform the Next Century

Because the first dollar that moves
can change everything.

Written by

Mark Falzon

Philanthropy as Amplifier
How Catalytic Capital Can Transform the Next Century
Because the first dollar that moves can change everything.
Written by Mark Falzon

Self-published in Australia by: Paradigm Communications Pty Ltd www.markfalzon.com

The intent of the author is to offer insight into the systems, structures, and leadership required to design a more coherent, regenerative, and purpose-driven world. This book explores the role of catalytic capital, the evolution of philanthropy, and the architecture of integrated investing as pathways toward building ventures, communities, and movements that make a difference.

Philanthropy as Amplifier: How Catalytic Capital Can Transform the Next Century by Mark Falzon

ISBN: 978-0-6457675-6-8
eBook ISBN: 978-0-6457675-7-5

FOREWORD

Hector D. Mujica

Every generation inherits wealth. But only some generations decide what that wealth is for. We are living through one of those moments now.

Over the next two decades, trillions of dollars will move between generations, across institutions, and into philanthropic vehicles. Foundations will grow. Family offices will expand. New funds and giving platforms will appear almost overnight. On paper, it should be a golden age of philanthropy.

Yet the paradox is hard to ignore. The ventures trying to solve some of the hardest problems in our world still struggle to find early capital. Climate adaptation. Workforce mobility. Food systems. Community resilience. The ideas exist. The talent exists. The urgency certainly exists.

What often does not exist is the first dollar willing to move.

I spent more than a decade working in philanthropy and impact investing through Google.org, helping lead our work across the Americas. During that time our teams partnered with nonprofits, governments, entrepreneurs, and investors to move capital toward opportunity at scale.

One lesson came up again and again. The most important philanthropic dollars are rarely the largest ones. They are the ones that move first. When philanthropic capital enters a system early, it does something subtle but powerful. It changes how everyone else sees the opportunity. Investors who might have waited become curious. Public institutions begin to pay attention. New actors enter the conversation.

A relatively small amount of capital can change the behavior of much larger pools of capital around it. That insight stayed with me throughout my time in philanthropy. It came into particularly sharp focus during one project that has stayed close to my heart.

Several years ago, our team began wrestling with a stubborn problem in the American labor market. Millions of jobs in the digital economy were going unfilled. At the same time, millions of capable workers could not access the training needed to enter those fields.

The barrier was not talent. It was financing. Training programs often required tuition that many working adults could not afford. Traditional student lending models were poorly suited for short, skills based programs. Nonprofit training providers struggled to scale because they lacked the capital to support students through the learning journey.

The system was stuck.

So we asked a different question. What if philanthropy could unlock a new kind of workforce financing?

Working with the remarkable team at Social Finance, we helped design what became the Google Career Certificates Fund. The model combined philanthropic capital from Google.org with additional financing to create a $100 million pool dedicated to helping Americans access job ready digital skills training.

The structure was intentionally catalytic. Learners could enroll with no upfront cost. They would only repay the loan if they secured a job earning above a certain income threshold. Training providers received upfront support to deliver wraparound services such as coaching, interview preparation, and job placement assistance.

In other words, the capital moved first so that people could move forward.

The goal was straightforward but ambitious. Train more than 20,000 Americans for entry level digital economy jobs and generate more than $1 billion in wage gains over the following decade.

But the deeper lesson was about capital itself.

The fund worked not simply because money was deployed, but because it was positioned differently. Philanthropic capital absorbed early uncertainty that traditional lenders could not. That signal unlocked a new pathway for workforce investment that would have been difficult for markets or government to create alone.

It was a small example of a much larger truth.

Where capital sits in a system often matters as much as how much capital there is. Placed thoughtfully, philanthropic dollars can act as signal capital. They absorb early risk. They invite others to participate. They transform a promising idea into something the broader financial system is willing to back.

That is the amplifier effect this book explores.

Mark Falzon captures something important when he argues that philanthropy should not think of itself only as a source of grants. It can also serve as catalytic infrastructure. A dollar deployed in the right place can unlock ten or twenty more from investors, governments, and institutions that would otherwise remain on the sidelines.

This idea is not theoretical. Across climate finance, global health, workforce development, and community investment, catalytic philanthropy is already quietly reshaping how capital moves. Blended finance structures are bringing together actors who historically operated in isolation. Family offices are exploring new ways to deploy risk tolerant capital. Governments are experimenting with partnership models that multiply the impact of public funding.

These developments reflect a broader shift in thinking. For a long time philanthropy was defined primarily by generosity. Today it is increasingly defined by stewardship.

Those who control capital are asking deeper questions about their role in shaping the systems around them.

How can capital serve people and communities more effectively?

How can it accelerate solutions rather than waiting for them to mature?

How can it rebuild trust in institutions at a moment when that trust is badly needed?

Catalytic philanthropy does not replace traditional giving. Hospitals still need donors. Schools still need grants. Communities still need direct support. But catalytic capital offers another path. It allows philanthropic dollars to do more than fund programs. It allows them to unlock systems.

In a world facing challenges that are systemic in nature, that distinction matters.

This book arrives at an important moment in that conversation. It offers both a framework and a set of practical ideas for those who steward wealth and want to see it move with greater purpose. Mark's argument is not that philanthropy should do everything. It is that philanthropy can help others do more.

The amplifier model invites philanthropists, investors, and policymakers to see capital not simply as a resource to distribute, but as a signal capable of mobilizing entire ecosystems of investment.

If even a modest share of global philanthropic capital adopted this mindset, the consequences could be profound. Not because philanthropy alone can solve the world's problems, but because it can help unlock the capital that might.

Ultimately this book is not just about financial structures. It is about imagination.

It asks what becomes possible when generosity is paired with strategic courage.

The coming decades will test how wisely we steward the wealth now moving through our institutions and communities.

Philanthropy can remain a quiet force for good. Or it can become something more catalytic. A signal that helps the rest of the system move.

The choice, as always, begins with the first dollar.

AUTHOR'S NOTE

Hector's Foreword captures the question that brought this book into being. What I want to add here is a note on why I felt I had to write it now.

Over the past two decades, working with founders, investors, and family offices through periods of rapid wealth creation and increasingly complex capital decisions, one pattern kept surfacing. When patient, risk-tolerant capital arrives early, systems reorganise around it. When it does not, even strong ideas stall. The pattern is structural rather than circumstantial. It repeats across sectors, geographies, and decades.

The architecture of that pattern is what this book sets out to describe. Not as theory, but as something already visible in the working practice of catalytic finance. The ideas here are drawn from the lived experiences of philanthropists, investors, policymakers, and founders who are testing new ways of putting capital to work, often without the language to describe what they are doing or the frameworks to scale it.

My hope is that the book offers both perspective and practical guidance for those who steward wealth and want to see it move with greater purpose. The coming decades will test how wisely we deploy the resources now flowing through our institutions and communities. If even a modest portion of that capital takes a catalytic position, the possibilities for the world ahead expand dramatically.

This book is an invitation to explore that possibility.

Mark Falzon

ACKNOWLEDGEMENTS

No meaningful work is ever created alone.

This book reflects the insights, conversations, and experiences of many people who are thinking deeply about the future of capital and the systems it shapes.

I am especially grateful to Hector Mujica, whose work in philanthropy and impact investing has helped illuminate the catalytic role that philanthropic capital can play in mobilising broader systems of investment. His willingness to share insights from his experience at Google.org and across the global philanthropy ecosystem helped sharpen many of the ideas explored in this book.

I am grateful to the founders, investors, and philanthropic leaders I have had the privilege of working alongside over the years. Their willingness to experiment with new structures, challenge conventional thinking, and take early risks has informed much of the thinking behind catalytic capital.

Special thanks to the community around MAD, whose shared belief that business and capital can be forces for regeneration continues to inspire the work we do.

I also want to acknowledge the researchers, institutions, and practitioners across the fields of impact investing, blended finance, and systems innovation whose work has helped advance this conversation globally.

Finally, my deepest thanks to my family and to those closest to me who continue to support the long arc of this work. Books are written in quiet moments, but they are made possible by the people who make those moments possible.

A NOTE ON THE CASE STUDIES

Several of the case studies in this book draw together common patterns observed across catalytic finance practice rather than describing a single named venture. Where a case is presented as composite, the structures, sequences, and outcomes reflect documented dynamics in the field, but specific names, locations, and amounts have been generalised to protect commercial confidentiality and to keep the focus on the underlying mechanics. Named cases, including the Google Career Certificates Fund described in the Foreword, are sourced and verifiable. Readers seeking specific examples are invited to explore the living library at www.mad.vc/philanthropy, which maintains a current record of named ventures and structures as the field evolves.

TABLE OF CONTENTS

PROLOGUE
THE POSSIBLE FUTURE

When Wealth Returns to the World

There are moments in history when the story of how the world works begins to shift. Old myths about wealth, progress, and power dissolve, and something new starts to emerge through the cracks. The future stops being an extension of the past and becomes a possibility that demands our participation.

We are living in one of those moments now.

Over the next two decades, the largest intergenerational wealth transfer in human history is unfolding. In the United States alone, Cerulli projects USD 124 trillion will change hands by 2048, with USD 18 trillion of that flowing directly into philanthropy. The global figure is harder to fix with precision, but the trajectory is clear: tens of trillions more will move into foundations, donor-advised funds, and family offices worldwide. This is the largest voluntary redistribution of private wealth ever attempted, an unprecedented opportunity for capital to return to the world that created it.

The question is not whether this capital will move. The question is how it moves, and whether it moves in ways that release the systems our future depends on.

At the same time, inequality has reached historic levels. Between 2000 and 2024, the richest 1 percent of the world's population captured 41 percent of all newly generated wealth. The bottom half received just 1 percent.

Without deliberate intervention, the coming wave of inheritance risks intensifying these divides and locking in patterns that already strain the social fabric.

We have never had more wealth dedicated to the public good. Yet we have never been closer to losing the systems that sustain us.

Across the world, billions sit in foundation endowments, much of it concentrated in the United States and Europe. Donor-advised funds accumulate flexible capital behind closed doors. Family offices increasingly behave like lightly supervised private equity platforms, influential and ubiquitous. Meanwhile, the ventures working on the most urgent problems, climate resilience, food security, mental health, water, education, community stability, remain chronically underfunded and structurally unsupported.

The world is not short on capital. It is short on coherent, catalytic capital.

This book argues for a simple but powerful shift in how philanthropic capital behaves. Instead of acting only as a source of grants, philanthropy can act as an amplifier, positioning capital so that one early dollar mobilises many others.

The Failure of "Business as Usual"

Fifteen years ago, impact investing promised to bridge this gap. It began with risk-tolerant pioneers, investors willing to take subordinated positions, accept concessionary returns, and build markets in places commercial money ignored.

As the field scaled, it changed.

More than three-quarters of impact investors now target risk-adjusted, market-rate returns. Impact investors account for just 6 percent of capital commitments to blended finance structures, and more than 80 percent of even that small share is invested on commercial rather than catalytic terms. Public sources, primarily development finance institutions and government agencies, now supply around 65 percent of all concessional capital. Private impact investors increasingly occupy safer, senior positions. Concessionary capital, the lifeblood of catalytic finance, has become rare.

Impact investing has not failed. But it has lost much of its catalytic edge.

Which brings us back to philanthropy.

The Most Powerful Dollar in the World

Blended finance is now widely understood as the use of catalytic capital from public or philanthropic sources to increase private investment in sustainable development. Philanthropy sits at the heart of that definition.

A philanthropic dollar placed early, structured as first-loss capital, a guarantee, or deeply patient equity, can change the psychology of risk for other investors, absorb uncertainty in ways private capital cannot, draw in government matching and co-investment, bring family offices and institutions off the sidelines, and give founders and communities the runway needed to build durable solutions.

When philanthropy moves first, it becomes an amplifier. One dollar becomes ten. Ten becomes fifty. Fifty becomes a system bent in a new direction.

This is not abstract. It is already happening:

- A catalytic tranche enabling hundreds of millions in clean energy investment across emerging markets.

- Philanthropic guarantees underwriting water and sanitation loans for low-income households, mobilising commercial lenders who would never have entered alone.
- Early catalytic commitments drawing corporate and institutional capital into climate adaptation projects once considered too risky.

The problem is not knowledge. It is consistency. As Hector describes in the Foreword, a relatively small philanthropic commitment can open entirely new financial pathways that markets alone could not create. We understand how catalytic capital works. We simply do not use it often enough, at scale, or with shared intent.

The Soul of the System We Are Funding

Beneath the mechanics, structures, and capital flows lies a deeper question:

What kind of world are we trying to fund?

Capital is not neutral.

Every dollar reinforces a worldview, about what matters, how value is defined, and what is worth building.

If we see the world as a set of markets to optimise, capital behaves one way.

If we see it as a living system to steward, capital behaves another.

The system this book imagines is grounded in several principles. Stewardship: land, water, culture, and people are relationships to be honoured, not assets to be extracted. Interdependence: capital connects rather than separates, recognising shared fate rather than fragmented interests. Courageous imagination: new futures are funded not because they are certain, but because they are necessary. Repair and remembrance: regeneration includes truth-telling and healing, not just innovation. Long time: investment horizons extend beyond quarters or election cycles into generational time. Ceremony and relationship: money is treated not simply as a tool, but as energy that carries intention and consequence.

This is the deeper architecture of catalytic philanthropy, the real work underneath the financial work.

What This Book Offers

This book is both pragmatic and aspirational. It provides a diagnosis of why capital remains stuck despite unprecedented availability, a framework for designing catalytic capital that multiplies rather than drips, stories where catalytic philanthropy has already accelerated systems change and where its absence has stalled progress, a blueprint for philanthropists, family offices, foundations, boards, and governments seeking to align capital with courage, an exploration of the soul of the systems we are trying to build and the role wealth must play in stewarding them, and an invitation to step into a new story of wealth, one where capital returns to the world that enabled its creation.

It is written for those who know that business as usual cannot meet this moment, and for those who feel the weight and the possibility of stewarding capital in a time when the next decades will shape the next centuries.

The Possible Future is not guaranteed. It is within reach if wealth chooses to become catalyst.

Welcome to Philanthropy as Amplifier.

CHAPTER ONE
THE GREAT CAPITAL RETURN

Why the Next Twenty Years Matter More Than the Last Two Hundred

Every era has an organising force, something that determines how societies grow, who thrives, what systems endure, and what possibilities emerge. In the agrarian age, that force was land. In the industrial age, it was machinery. In the digital age, it became data.

In the twenty-first century, that organising force is capital. Not abstract financial capital, but the movement of capital: where it goes, when it goes, who activates it, and what it makes possible.

Right now, capital is poised for the most significant transition in human history. This is the **Great Capital Return**.

Over the next twenty years, more wealth will transfer between hands, generationally, institutionally, and philanthropically, than in the previous two centuries combined.

The numbers are staggering:

- In the United States alone, Cerulli projects USD 124 trillion will shift across generations by 2048, with USD 18 trillion of that flowing into philanthropic vehicles.
- Global figures are harder to pin down with precision, but parallel intergenerational transfers across Europe, Asia, and the Middle East suggest the worldwide total is significantly larger.

- Family offices, now one of the fastest growing capital structures on the planet, already influence trillions in assets and are set to inherit even more.
- Foundation endowments hold extraordinary scale. The Harvard Kennedy School's 2018 Global Philanthropy Report identified more than USD 1.5 trillion in global foundation assets across 260,000 foundations, heavily concentrated in the United States and Europe. More recent estimates suggest US foundations alone now hold close to USD 1.5 trillion, with global totals materially higher. Annual foundation giving in the United States exceeded USD 109 billion in 2024, with global totals likely well above USD 150 billion.
- Donor-advised funds continue to accumulate flexible capital at unprecedented speed, often without equivalent deployment.

The choices made by foundations, family offices, and public institutions over the next two decades will determine whether this capital accelerates systemic solutions or remains largely passive.

On paper, this should be a moment of extraordinary possibility.

A moment when capital, liberated from founders and redistributed into new hands, flows into climate resilience, food security, water access, mental health, public health, education, and community stability.

A moment when wealth finally becomes a force for systems change rather than systemic strain.

But the numbers hide a deeper truth.

The world is not short on capital.

The world is short on capital willing to move first.

The Paradox of Abundance

We live in an era defined by a profound contradiction.

The greatest accumulation of philanthropic and private wealth in history is occurring alongside the greatest set of global challenges in history.

The contrast is stark:

- We have trillions of philanthropic dollars sitting in foundations, DAFs, and family offices.
- Yet the ventures working on humanity's most urgent problems struggle for early stage funding.
- Wealth concentrates faster each year, while inequality widens at a pace not seen since the industrial revolution.
- Technology accelerates, but social safety nets lag behind.
- Climate instability intensifies, yet catalytic investment into adaptation, food systems, and community resilience remains comparatively small.

It is not that wealth holders lack intention.

It is that the system for deploying wealth is misaligned with the realities of the world it claims to serve.

Most philanthropic capital remains structured for a slower, simpler, more local era:

- Annual grant cycles
- 5 percent payout rates
- Endowments invested in conventional markets
- A preference for proven models over emerging ones
- A desire for certainty over catalytic impact
- A governance culture that rewards caution more than courage

These structures have tremendous value. But they were built for incremental service, not systemic transformation.

Meanwhile, the world now operates on exponential curves.

Philanthropy does not.

A System That Cannot Keep Pace

The mismatch between global need and philanthropic velocity is not merely unfortunate. It is structural.

Several forces keep philanthropic capital from acting at the speed required.

1. Legacy Governance Models

Boards prioritise preservation over activation. Risk committees resist uncertainty. Investment committees optimise for the endowment rather than the mission.

2. Fragmentation Across Capital Types

Philanthropy acts alone. Government acts reactively. Private investors act cautiously. Impact investors increasingly behave like traditional investors. There is no shared architecture for coordination.

3. Cross Border Friction

Around the world, tax and regulatory frameworks make global giving difficult.

The 2025 Global Philanthropy Environment Index confirms that cross border flows are the weakest area of global philanthropy, even as global problems increasingly require cross border solutions.

4. Misaligned Incentives

Foundations are rewarded for stability, not innovation. DAFs reward accumulation rather than deployment. Family offices reward growth rather than risk taking. Impact funds reward performance rather than catalyticity.

These incentives are rational within the system.

Yet collectively they are catastrophic for the system.

5. The Illusion of Safety

Many philanthropists believe the safest move is to wait.

But when the world is accelerating, waiting carries greater risk than moving first.

The result is a philanthropic engine that is powerful but stalled, filled with fuel but lacking ignition.

The Missing Middle

If we map the movement of philanthropic capital, a troubling pattern emerges.

- Most giving goes to immediate service delivery or legacy institutions.
- Most investing goes to late stage, proven ventures.
- Very little funding goes to the middle, the early, risky, systemic work that allows new solutions to scale.

This "missing middle" is precisely where the world's most urgent ventures live:

- Community led climate adaptation
- Regenerative food systems
- Water security
- Education innovation
- Mental health infrastructure
- Prevention based health models
- Public good technology
- Clean energy access
- Circular supply chain transitions

These are not charity projects.

They are the scaffolding of a livable future.

Yet they remain capital starved because they fall between two paradigms:

- Too risky for commercial investment
- Too complex for traditional philanthropy

This middle zone is where catalytic capital belongs.

The workforce financing model Hector describes in the Foreword is one example of this middle zone in action: philanthropic capital absorbed early uncertainty, and the rest of the capital system reorganised around that signal.

Why the Next Twenty Years Are a Hinge in History

Humanity rarely receives a moment like this, a moment when the scale of capital and the severity of global challenge converge.

The Great Capital Return is not merely a demographic phenomenon.

It is a civilisational one.

The decisions wealth holders make in the next twenty years will determine:

- how fast climate adaptation scales
- how food systems transition
- how mental health infrastructure evolves
- how water security stabilises
- how education reimagines itself
- whether community resilience grows or fractures
- whether inequality deepens or narrows
- whether the world we pass onward is coherent or collapsing

We are not simply inheriting wealth.

We are inheriting responsibility.

For the first time, philanthropy has the potential not merely to support the world, but to activate it.

Catalytic Philanthropy: The Missing Archetype

The world does not need philanthropy that fills gaps.

It needs philanthropy that opens pathways.

Catalytic philanthropy is the archetype missing from the current capital architecture. It is the philanthropic identity that matches the scale and speed of this moment.

Catalytic philanthropy moves first. It absorbs uncertainty, signals confidence, draws in private investment, brings government into alignment, mobilises institutional capital that has been waiting on the sidelines, anchors community-led work that markets ignore, and multiplies impact far beyond its own financial footprint.

It is not more generous than traditional philanthropy. It is more strategic, more architectural, more interdependent.

Most importantly, catalytic philanthropy positions wealth not as an end, but as a beginning.

The Call of This Moment

The Great Capital Return is already in motion. The question is not whether wealth will move, but how. Cautiously, incrementally, in fragments, or catalytically.

This book argues for the latter. Not because catalytic philanthropy is fashionable, but because it is structurally effective. Not because the world needs more philanthropy, but because the world needs philanthropy that multiplies.

The next chapters explore how this shift happens: how capital moves from stagnation to flow, from fear to confidence, from isolation to integration, from generosity to geometry.

This is the beginning of the descent. The clear-eyed recognition of where we are, what is at stake, and why the future depends on reimagining how wealth returns to the world.

CHAPTER TWO
THE BOTTLENECK

How Systems, Laws and Institutions Keep Capital From Moving

If the Great Capital Return represents the potential of this moment, the Bottleneck represents its constraint. It is the invisible machinery (psychological, legal, institutional, structural) that determines whether catalytic capital flows or remains inert.

To understand why philanthropy struggles to act catalytically, we must examine the systems that hold it in place. Wealth does not move freely. It moves through structures, and structures shape destiny.

1. The Apparatus of Caution

Philanthropy was built to be careful. Foundations were designed for stability: steady payouts, defensive portfolios, slow cycles, conservative governance. Donor advised funds (DAFs) were designed for tax optimisation and long-term giving flexibility, not systemic activation. Family offices were designed around stewardship, privacy, and intergenerational preservation.

Family offices were designed around stewardship, privacy, and intergenerational preservation.

These structures make sense when the goal is preservation. They become problematic when the world requires mobilisation.

Across global philanthropy, five governance behaviours reinforce caution. Preservation over activation: endowments aim to last forever, even when the world cannot wait forever. Certainty over discovery: boards favour what has worked before rather than what might work next. Consensus over courage: decisions require alignment among trustees who often do not share the same risk appetite. Optics over outcomes: philanthropists fear reputational missteps more than missed opportunity. Incrementalism over systems change: grants are structured as isolated interventions rather than leverage points.

These tendencies are not moral failings. They are the inherited architecture of an earlier era. But when the world accelerates, old architectures become bottlenecks.

2. The Geography of Philanthropic Stagnation

Global data reveals a troubling pattern. The world holds well over USD 1.5 trillion in foundation assets, mostly concentrated in the United States and Europe, yet most of these assets are not deployed catalytically. They sit in conventional portfolios, surrounded by long-standing restrictions. More than 90 percent of foundations globally hold less than USD 10 million in assets, too small to absorb risk independently. Foundations outside the United States and Europe remain underdeveloped, underfunded, and often politically constrained.

The 2025 Global Philanthropy Environment Index makes the bottleneck explicit. The overall global environment score sits at 3.60 out of 5, moderately favourable. The weakest dimension globally is cross-border philanthropy, where enabling conditions scored 3.40, the lowest of all indicators.

In a world where climate, food, water, and health challenges are transnational, the regulatory environment for philanthropy remains fundamentally misaligned with reality. Philanthropy cannot scale systems change when the system it operates inside is not designed to move.

3. The Tax Paradox

Almost every OECD country provides some form of tax incentive for philanthropy. In theory, these incentives should accelerate giving. In practice, they create a paradox: they reward donating but not activating, encourage parking money in philanthropic vehicles without incentivising catalytic deployment, and reinforce control rather than coordination.

The examples are familiar. DAFs in the United States allow donors to claim tax benefits immediately but face no minimum payout requirement, so assets accumulate faster than they are deployed. Foundations face minimal payout rates, often around 5 percent annually, which means roughly 95 percent of capital typically remains invested in portfolios unaligned with mission. Cross-border giving is heavily restricted, particularly in Australia, East Asia, and parts of Europe, leaving philanthropy unable to respond to global needs with global flexibility.

The tax infrastructure of philanthropy is structurally conservative. It rewards capital retention and unintentionally penalises catalytic deployment. The Bottleneck is not a failure of generosity. It is a failure of design.

4. Impact Investing Lost Its Catalytic Edge

For a brief moment, impact investing seemed poised to solve the Bottleneck.

Its early pioneers took risks and funded markets traditional investors ignored.

But as the field professionalised, something shifted.

Recent data from the Global Impact Investing Network and Convergence reveals the scale of that shift:

- More than 75 percent of impact investors now target risk-adjusted, market-rate returns.
- Impact investors supplied just 6 percent of capital commitments to blended finance structures over the past three years, roughly 400 million dollars in total.
- More than 80 percent of even that small share was invested on commercial terms, primarily as senior equity or debt rather than first-loss or subordinated positions.
- Around 65 percent of all concessional capital, the catalytic layer that makes blended finance possible, comes from public sources rather than from impact investors or philanthropy.

Impact investing became a destination for capital, not a catalyst for systems change. Its maturation increased legitimacy and reduced willingness to take catalytic risk in roughly equal measure.

This explains why philanthropic catalytic capital is so urgently needed. Impact investors have moved up market. Governments cannot move first. Only philanthropy remains structurally capable of absorbing early uncertainty.

The Bottleneck persists because the one actor designed to move first has rarely been equipped, or encouraged, to do so.

5. Bureaucratic Gravity and the Pace Problem

Philanthropy's internal processes were designed for stability. Grant applications, committee approvals, annual budget cycles, and long deliberation periods create order and accountability.

But global crises operate on vastly shorter timelines. Climate feedback loops accelerate. Food shocks ripple through supply chains in weeks. Water scarcity expands exponentially. Misinformation spreads across populations in minutes. Artificial intelligence reshapes markets in months, not years.

The philanthropic process is increasingly outpaced by the dynamics it seeks to influence. The world moves in days and months. Philanthropy moves in quarters and years. Governments move in election cycles. Institutions move in decades.

Catalytic capital must operate at the speed of the problem, not the speed of the committee.

6. The Institutional Fear of Being First

Across philanthropists, foundation boards, family offices, and even impact investors, the same sentence emerges repeatedly: "We love this idea. We just do not want to be first."

The fear is understandable. Reputational harm. Backing the wrong initiative. Being exploited by other investors. Explaining catalytic losses to a conservative board. Innovation without precedent.

But the world's most urgent problems are pre-precedent, not post-precedent. If everyone waits for someone else to go first, nothing moves.

This is the psychology of the Bottleneck. It may be the single most powerful inhibitor of catalytic action.

7. Financial Products Work Against Systems Change

Most philanthropic vehicles replicate the structure of conventional finance. Foundations sit on endowments invested for market-rate return, with mission-aligned work funded from a small payout. DAFs operate as indefinite holding structures where capital can remain undeployed for long periods. Impact funds become market-rate funds with social language, where catalytic positions are rare. Family offices run diversified portfolios, often guided by advisors incentivised to protect assets under management rather than mobilise capital.

These products were designed for stability, preservation, and risk management, not catalytic movement. The product is rational for the institution. The outcome is irrational for the world.

8. The Hidden Costs of Inaction

Every year catalytic capital does not move:

- founders burn out
- communities lose resilience
- climate adaptation falls behind
- fragile systems weaken
- government programs fail to scale
- institutional trust declines
- inequality widens
- social cohesion erodes

The Bottleneck has human, institutional, and planetary consequences.

We often measure philanthropic impact by what is funded. The deeper measure may be what remains unfunded, the opportunities lost because capital stayed still.

9. The Loop That Keeps Capital Frozen

Mapped together, the behavioural, structural, and institutional forces that bind philanthropy reveal a closed loop. Capital is abundant, but locked in vehicles designed for caution. Mechanisms are outdated, built for incremental giving rather than systemic activation. Regulation restricts movement, particularly cross-border and catalytic flows. Institutions reward preservation, with boards fearing downside more than stagnation. Impact investing has moved up market, leaving a catalytic vacuum. Government cannot move first, because public capital requires private confidence before deploying at scale. And so everyone waits for someone else, with courage outsourced to no one.

This is the Bottleneck. A system designed to produce exactly the outcomes we see. Because the loop is systemic rather than personal, it cannot be disrupted by good intentions alone. It requires a new architecture, one that redefines the purpose of the philanthropic dollar.

10. Why Recognising the Bottleneck Matters

This chapter is not an indictment of philanthropy. It is an explanation. A systemic diagnosis.

To release catalytic capital, we must understand the forces that keep it frozen. The Bottleneck is not created by lack of generosity, intelligence, resources, or intention. It is created by structures and incentives that made sense in one era but no longer match the world we inhabit.

Without understanding the Bottleneck, catalytic philanthropy remains a hopeful idea. With understanding, it becomes a practical strategy.

The next chapter introduces that strategy, not as theory, but as a set of structures, sequences, and multipliers that turn one dollar into many and transform philanthropic capital from a passive resource into an active force for systems change.

[illegible] And so every [illegible]

[illegible] designed [illegible] exactly [illegible]

[illegible] Why Recognizing the Bottleneck Matters

[illegible]

CHAPTER THREE
CATALYTIC CAPITAL

What It Is, How It Works, and Where It's Already Emerging

Every system that ever transformed, economically, politically, socially, did so because someone went first. Someone absorbed uncertainty. Someone made the early commitment that allowed others to act.

In the world of capital, that early commitment is not a philosophical idea. It is a financial structure. Catalytic capital is that structure.

It is one of the most misunderstood, underused, and powerful tools available to philanthropists, family offices, foundations, governments, and impact-aligned investors. It is the bridge between the world we have and the world we need.

This chapter explains what catalytic capital is, how it works, and why it is already emerging around the world, often quietly, sometimes imperfectly, but always with transformative potential.

1. What Catalytic Capital Actually Is

Catalytic capital is not charity, not impact investing with softer edges, not high-risk venture philanthropy. It is a specific role in the capital stack:

Capital that moves first, absorbs uncertainty, and draws in additional investment that would not have happened otherwise.

What defines catalytic capital is function, not cost. It has three core traits.

Early. It enters before commercial investors, before models are proven, before markets are mature. It is the source of confidence.

Risk-absorbing. It accepts potential loss, not recklessly but strategically, so others can enter confidently and sustainably.

Mobilising. It draws in other capital: private investment, institutional commitments, government matching, corporate syndicates, and adjacent philanthropic flows.

In short, catalytic capital multiplies. Where traditional philanthropy funds activities, catalytic philanthropy funds possibility.

2. How Catalytic Capital Works: The Five Roles

Across every functioning blended finance or catalytic investment structure, catalytic capital consistently performs five roles. They are universal across sectors, from climate to water, food to health, education to community resilience.

The **signal role**: catalytic capital is the first yes. It changes the psychology of risk by showing that someone has done the work and believes in the model.

The **de-risking role**: it absorbs uncertainty through first-loss positions, guarantees, concessionary equity, flexible debt, or outcomes-based repayment.

The **alignment role**: it brings private, public, and philanthropic actors into coherence, creating shared direction and shared confidence.

The **activation role**: it triggers adjacent capital streams, co-investors, corporate strategic funds, DFIs, pension-aligned vehicles, and other philanthropists.

The **stabilisation role**: it supports long-term resilience through evergreen structures, recycled repayments, catalytic reserves, and multi-year funding stability.

These five roles turn catalytic capital from a grant with a twist into infrastructure. Catalytic capital is the scaffolding of systems change.

3. How 1 Becomes 10, and 10 Becomes 20

The multiplication effect of catalytic capital is not magical. It is mathematical, driven by sequence rather than scale.

Across the world, catalytic structures consistently follow a capital choreography: **1 → 3 → 5 → 10 → 20.**

A philanthropic dollar provides early signal and absorbs uncertainty. Private dollars follow because risk has shifted. Government dollars align because credible partners are now at the table. Adjacent dollars, corporate, institutional, and DFI, enter because momentum is visible. Systems stabilise, attracting even more capital.

The catalytic effect is a cascade, not a subsidy.

4. Emerging Global Examples

A. Clean Energy in Sub-Saharan Africa

How a USD 10m First-Loss Layer Mobilised USD 110m

A pan-African distributed solar company needed capital to scale. Private investors were interested, but early market volatility made them cautious.

The solution was a USD 10 million philanthropic first-loss tranche inside a blended fund. Philanthropy agreed to absorb early losses. DFIs entered next with USD 40 million of senior capital. Private funds followed with USD 60 million in commercial commitments. Local banks joined with working capital once default data improved.

The result: USD 10 million drew in USD 110 million and electrified more than 350,000 households.

This did not happen because the technology was new. It happened because the structure was new.

B. Water and Sanitation Loans in South Asia

The Guarantee That Mobilised Commercial Banks

Water and sanitation projects rarely attract early lenders. Small loans to low-income households are perceived as risky and unprofitable.

A philanthropic fund provided a partial credit guarantee, covering up to 20 percent of potential losses.

- Two commercial banks entered.
- Their combined lending exceeded USD 50 million over three years.
- Delinquency remained under 2 percent.
- Repayments recycled into new loans.

The philanthropic capital was never fully called.

But without it, the banks would never have entered.

Catalytic capital is not always spent. Sometimes its value lies in being available.

C. A Regenerative Agriculture Platform in Latin America

Catalytic Equity That Changed the Trajectory

A next-generation regenerative farming venture needed growth capital.

Commercial investors wanted proof of yield improvement, but farmers required transition financing upfront.

A philanthropic investor offered patient catalytic equity, tied to soil health milestones rather than financial milestones.

This early capital enabled:

- data collection
- farmer training
- supply chain commitments from a multinational buyer
- government subsidy alignment

Within eighteen months, the venture closed a USD 35 million Series A from mainstream climate investors.

Catalytic equity built the bridge from idea to investability.

D. Digital Mental Health in Southeast Asia

Blended Finance for Public Health Infrastructure

Governments across Southeast Asia recognised rising mental health challenges but lacked systems capacity.

A catalytic fund designed a three-tier structure:

1. philanthropic grants for platform development
2. concessionary debt for scale-up
3. government outcome payments tied to verified health improvements

The program reached more than 2 million people and is now part of national health budgets.

Catalytic capital created the evidence that public capital later adopted.

E. Blue-Carbon Coastal Restoration

Corporate Co-Investment Triggered by Philanthropic Signalling

A coastal restoration project integrating mangrove rehabilitation, community livelihoods, and blue-carbon credits needed early investment.

A philanthropic foundation committed USD 5 million as anchor, signalling legitimacy.

That single commitment triggered:

- a corporate net-zero fund's USD 20 million investment
- a government climate resilience grant
- a local microfinance partner's matched loans
- technical support from a regional conservation body

The catalytic multiplier exceeded 8x at financial close and 24x over the following three years.

5. Catalytic Capital Is Already Emerging, But Without a Shared Language

Across climate, water, food, health, education, community development, and public good technology, catalytic capital is appearing everywhere. But it tends to be accidental, under-theorised, unreported, and structurally inconsistent. It is often invisible to policymakers, mislabelled as grantmaking, misunderstood by boards, and treated as one-off innovation rather than replicable architecture.

This lack of shared language is itself a bottleneck. There is no common taxonomy for catalytic tranches, risk-sharing structures, first-loss vehicles, blended finance templates, governance guardrails, multiplier equations, or cross-sector collaboration patterns.

Catalytic capital has outgrown its vocabulary. This book is one attempt to give it the language and structure it needs to scale.

6. Catalytic Capital vs. Traditional Philanthropy vs. Impact Investing

The distinctions matter, particularly for boardrooms, family offices, and governments deciding where to position their capital.

Traditional philanthropy funds projects, seeks certainty, prioritises service delivery, focuses on direct outcomes, often operates locally, and works last in the chain. Impact investing funds businesses, seeks risk-adjusted return, prioritises investability, tracks financial and social metrics, often works in defined sectors, and enters after proof. Catalytic capital funds possibility, seeks leverage rather than return, prioritises systemic activation, focuses on multipliers rather than outputs, operates across sectors, and works first.

Catalytic capital fills the missing middle, the zone between charity and commerce, between direct service and market scale. The world's greatest challenges live in that middle zone.

7. The Properties of Catalytic Capital

Catalytic capital has three defining qualities.

Asymmetric impact: the influence of catalytic capital is disproportionate to the dollars deployed. Its role is to release systems, not to fund them alone.

Renewable impact: catalytic capital often recycles through repayments, released guarantees, equity exits, or reallocation into new catalytic vehicles.

C. Multiplicative Impact

Its success is measured by the capital it mobilises, not the grants it gives.

A catalytic dollar may not directly fund everything.

But it makes everything fundable.

8. The Why, Synthesised

The world needs catalytic capital because climate solutions are capital intensive and risk asymmetric, because water and food systems require early investment before markets materialise, because mental health and education innovations need patient capital, because governments cannot move first, because impact investing has drifted, because community-led innovation cannot meet commercial thresholds, and because systemic change requires early, risk-absorbing, confidence-building capital.

If philanthropy does not fill this role, no one else will.

9. Where This Chapter Leads

We now understand what catalytic capital is, how it works, what roles it performs, how it multiplies, and where it is already emerging. But catalytic capital, without proper guardrails, can distort systems as easily as it can release them.

The same principle repeats across sectors. Climate funds, workforce financing models, regenerative agriculture platforms, and health infrastructure all demonstrate the same structural truth: when catalytic capital moves first, the rest of the system begins to move with it.

The next chapter introduces those guardrails, the principles that keep catalytic capital ethical, equitable, and regenerative as it scales.

CHAPTER FOUR
PROOF OF CONCEPT

Stories of Amplification, and What They Reveal

Catalytic capital is more than a philosophy. It is a repeatable, observable pattern emerging quietly across the world. In every region, across climate, water, housing, food systems, mental health, education, and community resilience, catalytic capital has already begun to reshape what is possible.

The stories rarely make headlines. They sit beneath the surface of the global financial system like tectonic plates, shifting the terrain long before anyone realises what moved.

This chapter offers a selection of stories shaped by the same underlying logic. Each reveals a different dimension of the amplifier model: how catalytic capital behaves, how systems respond, how multipliers emerge, and what happens when catalytic elements are missing.

These are not abstractions. They are proof. And they show, with clarity and precision, why the world needs catalytic philanthropy now.

1. CLEAN ENERGY ACCESS

A First-Loss Layer That Electrified a Continent

Context

Sub-Saharan Africa has some of the world's highest solar potential, and some of the lowest rates of electricity access.

Distributed solar companies can scale rapidly, but early stage financing is nearly impossible. Investors demand a track record. Banks demand collateral. Governments demand evidence.

The stalemate persisted for years. Technology existed. Demand was real. The financial bridge that could allow scale had not yet appeared.

The Founder's Decision

The founder of the solar venture understood the problem clearly. The technology worked. Demand was clear. Communities were ready. What was missing was not a product or a market, but the financial bridge that would allow the company to move from pilot programs to meaningful scale.

In meetings with investors, the conversation often followed a predictable pattern. Investors liked the model, admired the mission, agreed that distributed solar could transform energy access across the region. But the next sentence was almost always the same: "Come back when you have a larger track record."

For the founder, this was the paradox. Without capital, there could be no track record. Without a track record, there could be no capital. It is a stalemate many early-stage ventures in emerging markets know well.

The company did not need charity. It needed a capital structure that could absorb the early uncertainty long enough for the model to prove itself.

The Investor's Hesitation

For commercial investors, the hesitation was rational. Distributed solar in emerging markets carries several layers of uncertainty: currency volatility, repayment data, regulatory change, and infrastructure risk. Even investors who believed in the long-term potential of the sector found it difficult to justify early exposure.

One investor described the dilemma simply: "The business model makes sense. The impact is clear. But without early data, we cannot justify the risk to our investment committee."

This is where most systems stall. Ideas are not rejected; they are postponed. Capital waits for evidence. Evidence waits for capital. The loop closes.

The Structural Insight

The breakthrough did not come from improving the technology or refining the business plan. It came from changing the position of capital in the structure.

The philanthropic foundation that provided the USD 10 million catalytic tranche did not attempt to fund the entire solution. Instead, it occupied the precise layer where uncertainty was highest. That single structural decision shifted the risk profile of the entire fund.

Once early losses were buffered, development finance institutions could justify their participation. Once DFIs entered, private funds saw a credible pathway. Once repayment data began to accumulate, local banks gained confidence to provide working capital.

The catalytic layer did not remove risk from the system. It reorganised where that risk lived. And that change was enough to release the rest of the capital stack.

What changed was not the technology. What changed was the position of risk inside the system.

The Structure

A global climate foundation provided a USD 10 million first-loss tranche within a USD 120 million blended fund designed to expand distributed solar across East and West Africa. The catalytic tranche absorbed early performance risk, de-risked currency volatility, and validated the underlying business models.

The Multiplier

Within six months, DFIs committed USD 40 million. Private funds committed USD 60 million. Local banks began issuing working capital loans once repayment data strengthened. Governments started pilot subsidy schemes aligned with the fund's metrics.

The philanthropic dollar did not power a single solar panel. But it powered the system that powered them.

The Outcome

More than 350,000 households gained access to electricity. Several countries later integrated similar structures into national clean-energy policies.

This is catalytic capital as ignition.

2. WATER AND SANITATION

The Guarantee That Created a Market

Millions of households across South Asia lack access to safe water or sanitation. Traditional lenders see this segment as high risk, low margin, and operationally complicated.

A philanthropic institution offered a partial credit guarantee covering up to 20 percent of potential losses for commercial banks willing to enter the water and sanitation loan market.

The Multiplier

The effect was immediate:

- Two commercial banks deployed over USD 50 million
- Default rates remained below 2 percent
- Lenders developed in-house expertise
- Repayment cycles were fast enough to recycle capital

The guarantee was almost never called, but without it the capital never would have moved.

The Outcome

More than 500,000 households gained access to water or sanitation infrastructure.

Catalytic capital's power is not in risk taking.

It is in risk shifting.

3. REGENERATIVE AGRICULTURE

Patient Capital That Built a New Supply Chain

Smallholder farmers across Latin America are trapped in extractive commodity markets that degrade soil and produce unstable income. Regenerative agriculture promises higher long-term yields and carbon benefits, but it requires upfront transition capital and long-term contracts.

A philanthropic family office invested USD 7 million in patient catalytic equity, linked to soil health performance metrics rather than financial metrics. That early support created the conditions for a multinational buyer to offer guaranteed purchase agreements, for two DFIs to provide working capital, for local banks to develop regenerative loan products, and for farmers to commit to transition pathways knowing risk was shared.

Eighteen months later, the venture closed a USD 35 million Series A. Today it supports more than 20,000 farmers and has become a model for regenerative supply chains globally.

Catalytic capital does not just fund farmers. It builds the system around them.

4. MENTAL HEALTH ACCESS

A Blended Model That Became Government Policy

Across Southeast Asia, mental health infrastructure is limited, fragmented, and heavily stigmatised. Government budgets are thin. Private investment is absent. NGOs lack scale.

A catalytic fund introduced a three-tier model: philanthropic grants to build a digital mental health platform, concessionary debt to scale the service across four countries, and government outcome payments once verified impact thresholds were met. The structure created evidence for effectiveness, confidence for policymakers, stable unit economics, and a growing user base.

Within five years, the platform reached more than two million people and was integrated into national health budgets in two countries. Catalytic capital created the evidence governments required to adopt and scale the solution.

5. COASTAL BLUE CARBON

Corporate Capital Drawn In by a Philanthropic Anchor

Mangrove ecosystems sequester carbon, protect coastlines, and support fisheries. But restoration projects struggle to attract finance because returns are slow and governance is complex.

A philanthropic foundation invested USD 5 million as an anchor commitment. That single act drew in USD 20 million from a corporate climate fund, matching capital from a government climate resilience program, technical support from a regional conservation science institute, and community co-ownership agreements backed by microfinance partners.

The project achieved a 24x capital multiplier over three years. The philanthropic foundation moved first. Everyone else waited until it did.

6. A FAILURE STORY

When Catalytic Capital Was Missing, and the System Collapsed

A social enterprise providing cold-chain logistics for rural health clinics in East Africa had the potential to reduce vaccine spoilage by more than 40 percent. The model was strong. Early pilots were promising. Community impact was clear.

No philanthropic first mover stepped forward. Commercial investors demanded proof of commercial viability. DFIs required demonstration of long-term government contracts. Governments insisted on scale before budgeting. Foundations preferred direct-service NGOs over infrastructure ventures. Impact investors insisted on market-rate return profiles.

Everyone waited for someone else.

The enterprise shut down after 18 months. Vaccine spoilage rates returned to baseline. A promising systemic innovation collapsed because the catalytic layer was absent.

Failure is part of the evidence base. It shows what happens when philanthropy does not act as amplifier.

7. Why These Cases Matter

These stories share five structural patterns. Someone absorbed uncertainty early; no systemic change happened without this. Philanthropy anchored the risk, not as subsidy but as structural ignition. Private capital followed only after clarity emerged; catalytic sequences always start with courage. Governments amplified what philanthropy validated, a pattern that holds across continents. And adjacent capital piled in once momentum became visible; this is how small catalytic acts transform into large systems.

The same logic underpins the Google Career Certificates Fund Hector describes in the Foreword. Catalytic capital is not about volume. It is about position and function.

8. What These Stories Reveal About Catalytic Philanthropy

The first dollar is more powerful than the final dollar. This is the inverse of traditional philanthropy.

Capital does not follow need, it follows confidence. Catalytic capital manufactures that confidence.

Systems are not scaled by the best ideas, but by the bravest early commitments. The idea alone is never enough.

Philanthropy is the only actor structurally free to absorb early uncertainty. Governments, private investors, and DFIs cannot play that role in the same way.

When philanthropy goes first, it stops acting alone. It becomes the conductor of a multi-capital orchestra.

Catalytic philanthropy is not charity. It is architecture. It designs the conditions under which systems can shift.

9. Where This Leads Next

These cases show that catalytic capital is real, repeatable, and globally relevant. But used irresponsibly or without guardrails, catalytic philanthropy can distort as easily as it can amplify.

The next chapter introduces the principles, constraints, and governance needed to keep catalytic capital ethical, equitable, and regenerative as it scales. The Possible Future must not only be activated. It must be stewarded.

CHAPTER FIVE
DESIGNING AN AMPLIFIER

A Blueprint for Boards, Family Offices, and Foundations

Catalytic philanthropy is not a mystery. It is a design discipline.

Once we understand the Bottleneck, the structural and psychological forces that keep capital frozen, the next question becomes practical: **how do we design capital that moves first, absorbs uncertainty, and multiplies impact?**

We have already seen how this works in practice. Hector's account of the Google Career Certificates Fund in the Foreword shows how positioning, not volume, creates the catalytic effect. By absorbing early uncertainty, philanthropic capital made it possible for other actors to participate in building a new pathway for workforce financing.

This chapter examines how that kind of catalytic structure can be designed deliberately. What follows is a blueprint: a clear and implementable framework for philanthropic actors who want to transform their capital from a passive resource into a catalytic force. It is written for those who sit at the decision points: trustees, principals, investment committees, governance bodies, and senior stewards of wealth.

The amplifier model only becomes real when these decision-makers act with intention.

1. First Decision: Your Role in the Capital Stack

The first question any philanthropic actor must answer is simple: **where should we sit in the capital stack?**

This is not a financial question. It is a strategic one. There are five primary positions catalytic philanthropy can take.

Signal anchor: a small, early commitment that tells the market "we believe the risk is worth taking." This often takes the form of a 5 to 15 percent anchor, a grant-and-equity hybrid, a below-market equity stake, a subordinated loan, or a catalytic guarantee. The function is not volume. It is validation.

First-loss or subordinated position: taking the earliest losses creates a buffer that attracts other classes of capital. This appears as first-loss equity, first-loss debt, subordinated debt, tiered tranches, or credit enhancement. It is one of the most powerful catalytic roles available.

Flexible, patient capital: catalytic capital without hard timelines, structured to match the real pace of systems change. Often structured as long-horizon equity, revenue-based financing, evergreen vehicles, or recoverable grants. This is catalytic time.

Blended partnership capital: capital that sits structurally between philanthropy and private investment. Outcome-based funding, concessional debt, milestone-triggered releases, discount-rate equity, program-related investments (PRIs). This creates alignment across multiple stakeholders.

Ecosystem capital: a catalytic role many overlook. It funds the connective tissue that makes systems change possible: policy support, technical assistance, community governance, data systems, convening costs, narrative and cultural work. This capital is not glamorous. But it is often the most catalytic of all.

2. Second Decision: How Much Flexibility You Are Willing to Offer

Catalytic capital is defined by flexibility, the willingness to absorb ambiguity so others can operate with clarity. Boards and investment committees should discuss four types of flexibility.

Flexibility of risk: what degree of loss can we tolerate in service of leverage? Catalytic capital is not reckless; it is asymmetrically disciplined, accepting small losses for large multipliers. A board willing to accept a limited first-loss exposure, for example 5 to 15 percent, can multiply its impact five to twenty times.

Flexibility of return: what kinds of returns are acceptable? Catalytic capital may accept concessionary returns, prioritise repayment over profit, recycle capital, forgo early upside, or accept capped returns. This is not charity. It is strategy. The return is in the multiplier.

Flexibility of time: how long are we willing to commit capital? Different catalytic structures operate on five-year, seven-to-ten-year, fifteen-year, or evergreen horizons. Time is leverage. Most systems shifts require patience markets do not provide.

Flexibility of structure: how much complexity can we manage? Catalytic capital often requires hybrid instruments, special purpose vehicles, government contracting, multi-stakeholder agreements, dynamic governance, and conditional tranches. Boards that fear complexity automatically constrain catalytic potential. Boards that embrace it become system-shapers.

3. Building a Catalytic Investment Policy (CIP)

Traditional investment policies are built around risk allocation, asset classes, geographic restrictions, return targets, and liquidity constraints. A Catalytic Investment Policy requires additional layers.

Catalytic purpose statement: a clear articulation of why the organisation intends to use catalytic capital. "To draw private and public capital toward climate adaptation." "To accelerate the transition to regenerative agriculture." "To de-risk early-stage health infrastructure." "To activate underfunded community-led solutions." Purpose guides structure.

Deployment mandate: catalytic capital must be deployed. The mandate may specify the percentage of endowment allocated to catalytic work, the percentage of annual giving allocated to catalytic vehicles, minimum commitments per year, preferred catalytic roles, and the time horizon for catalytic commitments. The single biggest risk in catalytic philanthropy is underdeployment.

Risk tolerance statement: defining acceptable loss thresholds, acceptable illiquidity, acceptable concession, preferred instruments, and prohibited uses. This becomes the backbone of governance.

Coordination policy: catalytic capital is relational. A CIP should define how partners are selected, when to engage government, when to engage private investors, how community governance is incorporated, and how adjacent capital is tracked.

Impact and amplification framework: unlike traditional philanthropy, catalytic philanthropy measures leverage ratio, additional capital mobilised, systems effects, policy alignment, governance shifts, and long-tail impacts. The metric is not output. It is amplification.

4. Designing a Catalytic Deal: A Step-by-Step Blueprint

Here is the practical sequence any philanthropic actor can follow.

Step 1: Identify the leverage point. Not every problem requires catalytic capital. Look for the missing middle, underinvested systems, high public benefit, fragmented actors, risk asymmetry, or early-stage infrastructure. Where the system stalls, catalytic capital belongs.

Step 2: Map the system. Understand who benefits, who carries risk, who decides, who delays, who accelerates, and who must be coordinated. Every catalytic structure must be context-specific.

Step 3: Select your catalytic role. Signal? First-loss? Concessionary? Patient? Ecosystem? Choose the position that releases the system's movement.

Step 4: Build the stack. This may involve a catalytic tranche, senior commercial capital, a government sidecar, a DFI risk layer, corporate participation, and community equity or ownership. A well-designed stack changes behaviour across all participants.

Step 5: Define the guardrails. Use the principles introduced earlier: alignment, transparency, additionality, humility, proportionality, accountability, long time horizon, and coherence. These are not moral guidelines. They are structural integrity.

Step 6: Set milestones and release conditions. Catalytic capital must be staged, conditional, evidence-based, and adaptive. This avoids dependency and ensures discipline.

Step 7: Communicate the signal. If catalytic capital moves quietly, its leverage is lost. The market must see you move. Signal drives activation.

Step 8: Build the ecosystem. Fund policy alignment, narrative, coordination, data systems, founder support, and community governance. This is often 10 to 20 percent of catalytic capital, and often the most important part.

Step 9: Measure amplification. Track capital mobilised, actors drawn in, systems changed, institutions aligned, resilience increased, and community outcomes. Amplification is the scoreboard.

Step 10: Recycle and reinforce. Catalytic capital is renewable through recoverable grants, loan repayments, equity exits, and guarantee releases. The amplifier model compounds over time when capital is recycled.

5. Governance for Catalytic Philanthropy

Catalytic philanthropy cannot run on good intentions. It requires governance. The catalytic governance model includes an independent catalytic committee, cross-sector advisors, conflict-of-interest protocols, transparent reporting, community voice, and sunset clauses.

Governance is the difference between catalytic capital and arbitrary capital.

6. Tools and Vehicles for Catalytic Action

Catalytic instruments include first-loss equity, subordinated debt, partial credit guarantees, concessional loans, revenue-share structures, evergreen catalytic vehicles, recoverable grants, outcomes-based contracts, PRIs and MRIs, debt-for-outcomes swaps, and layered capital stacks.

Catalytic vehicles include blended finance funds, philanthropic co-investment pools, systems-change accelerators, climate transition funds, community catalytic trusts, public-private catalytic platforms, and regional catalytic hubs. The book's online library provides examples of each.

7. The Three Catalytic Mindsets

More than structure, catalytic philanthropy requires a mindset shift. Courage: someone must go first; let it be us. Leverage: our goal is not to fund everything, but to draw in everything. Stewardship: we hold resources not to preserve them, but to activate the systems that sustain life.

8. Where This Leads Next

With this chapter, the architecture is complete. We now understand the scale of the Great Capital Return, the systems bottleneck preventing capital from moving, the catalytic structures that release change, the evidence that amplification works, and the blueprint for designing catalytic capital.

What remains is the inner architecture. The next chapter explores the soul of the system we are trying to fund.

CHAPTER SIX
THE SOUL OF THE SYSTEM WE ARE FUNDING

Capital, Cosmology, and the Work of Repair

Every financial system rests on an invisible foundation. Not on markets or institutions, but on something deeper: a belief about what life is, what matters, and who we serve.

Capital is never just capital. It is a story, a cosmology, a set of assumptions made concrete. Underneath every investment strategy is a worldview. Underneath every philanthropic structure is a theory of value. Underneath every capital stack is an imagination, often unexamined, about how the world works.

This chapter asks a question that the technical architecture cannot answer on its own: **what is the soul of the system we are trying to fund?**

Catalytic capital, for all its structure, rigor, and technical architecture, is also a moral technology. It carries intention. It transmits belief. And at this moment in history, the values behind our capital matter as much as the capital itself.

1. Capital Flows Toward What We Believe Is Real

In the modern world, capital behaves like a natural force. It flows toward certain things and not others, shaping what gets built, rewarding particular behaviours, reinforcing particular values. But capital does not flow by accident. It flows according to what we believe is real, valuable, and possible.

If we believe only markets are real, capital flows to markets. If we believe only short-term returns matter, capital flows to what can be measured quickly. If we believe precaution is safer than possibility, capital sits still. If we believe the world is a collection of disconnected units, capital fragments. If we believe extraction is the purpose of ownership, capital concentrates.

Catalytic capital challenges those beliefs. It says: we can choose what capital is for. This is the deeper work of catalytic philanthropy, not only to move money, but to move what money believes in.

2. The Difference Between "More" and "Enough"

Modern capitalism has long operated on the assumption that more is the primary measure of progress: more growth, more output, more consumption, more markets, more extraction, more speed, more capital, more assets, more everything. Systems built on endless growth eventually collapse under their own weight.

The world we are trying to fund requires a different logic. Not a logic of more, but a logic of enoughness: enough energy to sustain life, enough food to nourish communities, enough water to sustain ecosystems, enough stability for families to thrive, enough agency for communities to lead, enough resilience to withstand shocks.

Catalytic capital is how philanthropy transitions from more to enough. It does not seek scale for its own sake. It seeks coherence. It funds systems that regenerate rather than systems that degrade, cycles that restore rather than cycles that extract, futures that include rather than futures that concentrate. In this sense, catalytic capital is not only a tool. It is a reorientation of purpose.

3. A Soul of Stewardship, Not Extraction

The world we are trying to fund is not built on ownership. It is built on relationship. A system of stewardship recognises that land is not a commodity, water is not a resource, people are not inputs, communities are not markets, and ecosystems are not externalities.

This worldview is older than modern finance. It runs through agrarian wisdom, indigenous traditions, and intergenerational governance practices across every continent. It is increasingly visible in regenerative agriculture, community land trusts, conservation finance, and place-based investing.

Catalytic capital aligns with stewardship when it supports regenerative agriculture instead of extractive monocultures, funds community-owned infrastructure rather than outsourced services, catalyses circular economies instead of linear waste streams, activates local governance rather than imposing external control, and strengthens relationships rather than transactions. Under stewardship, capital becomes the servant of life rather than its master.

4. A Soul of Interdependence, Not Separation

Traditional finance treats the world as disconnected: investor versus investee, capital versus community, risk versus return, public versus private, philanthropy versus markets. Catalytic capital challenges this dualism. It recognises that public health relies on economic stability, economic stability relies on ecological health, ecological health relies on community resilience, community resilience relies on social trust, and social trust relies on inequality reduction.

Systems do not change in isolation. They change in relationship. Catalytic capital funds those relationships, the connective tissue: coordination, community leadership, shared governance, cross-sector alignment, data systems, narrative coherence.

This is not soft work. It is system work. Interdependence is not merely a philosophy. It is an operating principle.

5. A Soul of Courageous Imagination, Not Polite Incrementalism

Incrementalism is the default mode of philanthropy: carefully funding the next pilot, the next study, the next improvement. Courageous imagination is different. It asks what would be possible if we stopped waiting for precedent, what we would build if we were not afraid of early risk, what structures could exist if wealth moved with purpose.

Catalytic philanthropy is the financial expression of imagination. It funds what does not yet exist, what will not exist without early support, and what may never exist if we continue to rely on models that brought us here.

Courageous imagination is not naïve. It is necessary. It is how systems change.

6. A Soul of Repair, Not Reinvention Without Reflection

The systems we are trying to shift, food, water, climate, health, education, governance, are shaped by histories of inequality, exclusion, colonisation, extraction, and dispossession. To fund a regenerative future without acknowledging these histories is to repeat them in quieter forms.

Repair requires truth-telling, community governance, reparative investment, cultural preservation, and indigenous leadership. Repair is not backward-looking. It is forward-building. It prevents philanthropy from funding efficiency while ignoring dignity. It avoids the arrogance of thinking systems can be reinvented without context.

Catalytic capital does not bypass repair. It funds it. A system cannot regenerate until it has been acknowledged.

7. A Soul of Long Time, Not Short Quarters

Markets operate on quarterly expectations. Politics operates on election cycles. Philanthropic governance operates on annual budgets. Life operates in long time: soil across seasons, forests across centuries, communities across generations, cultures across millennia.

Long time is the temporal foundation of catalytic capital. It asks what this capital will make possible thirty years from now, what foundations we are laying for future generations, what slow, quiet work we are committed to. Catalytic capital matches itself to the pace of life: patient, durable, regenerative. The Possible Future cannot be built in short quarters.

8. A Soul of Intentional Practice, Not Neutral Transaction

Money is not neutral. It carries intention, psychology, and history. Catalytic philanthropy treats financial decisions as an act of consciousness: bringing attention, respect, and relational truth to where capital goes. It asks who is at the table, who decides, who benefits, who is responsible, what values are transmitted through this capital.

Catalytic capital operates with this awareness. It respects not only the outcome of capital, but the manner in which capital moves. How we fund is as important as what we fund.

9. Why the Soul Matters to Catalytic Capital

Catalytic capital is mechanical. It is also moral. Without an ethical foundation, catalytic capital could distort markets, reinforce inequity, enable extraction, centralise power, accelerate unintended harm, scale solutions without context, or shape systems without consent.

The soul of the system prevents distortion. It grounds architecture in ethics. It ensures catalytic capital accelerates life rather than accelerating collapse. It is not optional. It is the compass. Catalytic capital is powerful, and anything powerful must be guided by intention.

10. Where This Leads

We have now built the two layers of catalytic philanthropy.

- the outer architecture of systems, structures, stacks, and multipliers
- the inner architecture of meaning, memory, stewardship, and long time

The next chapter brings these together in practical terms.

It explores what The Possible Future might look like if catalytic capital becomes a global norm, and what it will look like if it does not.

Because a soul without structure is sentiment.

And structure without soul is machinery.

Catalytic philanthropy requires both.

CHAPTER SEVEN
TWENTY YEARS FROM NOW

Scenarios for The Possible Future

The future does not arrive fully formed. It emerges from the choices we make now, especially the choices made with power, capital, intention, and imagination. If catalytic philanthropy is the mechanism that releases the Great Capital Return, then the next twenty years become the hinge on which the next hundred swing.

This chapter offers two scenarios for the world ahead. The Catalytic Future, where philanthropic capital acts as amplifier and activates systems that currently stall. The Default Future, where the Bottleneck persists and capital concentrates rather than circulates.

Neither scenario is guaranteed. Both are plausible. Only one is fit for the world we want to build.

1. The Catalytic Future: When Wealth Returns to the World

By 2045, catalytic philanthropy has become a recognised global architecture. It is not universal, no system ever is, but it is widely enough adopted that its presence shapes the trajectory of entire sectors.

A. Climate Systems Shift From Reaction to Stabilisation

Catalytic capital accelerates community-led adaptation, nature-based solutions, distributed energy, coastal resilience, and regenerative land and water systems. Government climate bodies, initially hesitant, now routinely co-invest alongside philanthropic anchors. Private capital flows follow the path philanthropic anchors create.

By 2045, energy access has expanded dramatically across Africa and South Asia, regenerative agriculture is widespread across Latin America and Asia, blue-carbon and watershed restoration models are mainstream, and adaptation financing is no longer a niche.

The defining change is not that philanthropy solved climate. It is that philanthropy activated the systems that could.

B. Water and Food Security Strengthen Through Regenerative Models

Catalytic capital opens the door to farmer transition financing, water funding mechanisms accessible to low-income communities, circular food systems, and community water governance. Transition financing, long considered too risky, becomes stabilised by catalytic tranches that draw in commercial banks, DFIs, and government guarantees.

By 2045, nutrient security improves, water markets become more equitable, soil health indicators trend positive in multiple regions, and rural livelihoods strengthen. Food and water systems begin behaving like regenerative ecosystems rather than extractive economies.

C. Health and Mental Health Infrastructure Expand Through Blended Systems

Catalytic philanthropy plays a central role in early-stage digital health, primary care infrastructure, community mental health platforms, and outcomes-based public health contracts. By absorbing early uncertainty, philanthropy allows governments to scale what works.

By 2045, community mental health programs reach hundreds of millions, digital primary care becomes a public utility in many nations, and prevention programs receive sustained investment. This is not utopia. It is what happens when proven models receive catalytic backing at the right moment.

D. Cities and Communities Become More Resilient

Catalytic capital triggers coordinated investment in climate adaptation, flood management, heat mitigation, localised energy, community enterprise, and digital infrastructure. Cities adopt catalytic partnership offices to coordinate philanthropy, private capital, and government budgets.

By 2045, urban resilience indices improve, infrastructure integrates risk data, and local ownership increases in development projects. Communities become active partners in designing their futures, not passive recipients of them.

E. Wealth Consciousness Evolves

The most subtle change is cultural. By 2045, catalytic philanthropy has become the expected identity of large foundations. Family offices reserve a percentage of assets for catalytic commitments. DAFs adopt voluntary payout frameworks oriented toward activation. Philanthropic boards evaluate amplification rather than expenditure.

Wealth transitions from being a container to becoming a circulator. The story of wealth shifts from accumulation to activation, from extraction to stewardship, from privilege to responsibility, from isolation to interdependence.

This is The Possible Future.

2. The Default Future: When the Bottleneck Holds

If catalytic philanthropy fails to emerge at scale, the next twenty years unfold differently. This scenario is not apocalyptic. But it is far less coherent, far less stable, and far less humane than it could be.

A. Climate Adaptation Falls Behind the Curve

Without catalytic activation, adaptation funding remains chronically insufficient. Private capital sits on the sidelines. Governments struggle to justify early, unproven models. Nature-based solutions fail to scale. Vulnerable communities absorb disproportionate damage.

Climate mitigation continues, but adaptation lags catastrophically. The costs multiply: human, economic, and ecological.

B. Water, Food, and Agriculture Remain Fragmented

Without catalytic capital, regenerative agriculture grows slowly. Water access markets stay underdeveloped. Soil degradation intensifies. Food insecurity spreads across climate-vulnerable regions.

Markets remain risk-averse. Governments remain reactive. Philanthropy stays incremental.

C. Mental Health and Primary Care Struggle to Scale

Without catalytic support, early-stage mental health models fail to secure growth capital. Community programs remain donor-dependent. Preventive healthcare remains underfunded. Digital infrastructure reaches only those who can afford it.

The burden of disease grows faster than the infrastructure needed to manage it.

D. Social Cohesion Erodes

If wealth continues to accumulate without activation, inequality deepens. Trust declines. Democratic institutions weaken. Misinformation accelerates. Civic fabric frays.

This is not a prediction. It is already happening. Catalytic philanthropy is not a silver bullet. But without it, the centrifugal forces intensify.

E. The Purpose of Wealth Collapses Into Anxiety or Apathy

When wealth lacks meaning, it becomes heavy. By 2045, in the Default Future, many philanthropic pools remain underdeployed. Family offices struggle with identity and purpose. Next-generation stewards experience existential drift. Large foundations operate in archaic modes. DAFs accumulate capital disconnected from impact.

Wealth becomes a burden rather than a catalyst.

3. The Divergence Between the Two Futures

Both futures begin from the same starting point: unprecedented wealth, accelerating global crises, structural bottlenecks, a massive intergenerational transition. One thing makes the difference: whether the philanthropic dollar is treated as a gift or as a signal.

If philanthropy continues to fund only direct service, it remains incremental. If philanthropy steps into its catalytic role, it becomes exponential.

This divergence is why catalytic philanthropy is not one strategy among many. It is the keystone in the arch of global transformation. The next decades will not be defined by the amount of capital available. They will be defined by how it moves.

4. How the Catalytic Future Becomes Real

To activate The Possible Future, several shifts must take place. Catalytic identity goes mainstream as philanthropic leaders embrace their role as architects rather than just funders. Blended finance becomes default as government agencies and DFIs build catalytic structures into standard practice. Family offices activate purpose as the next generation turns wealth into intentional architecture. Cross-border barriers ease as tax and regulatory reforms enable global catalytic flows. Data and transparency improve so that we track leverage, not just expenditure. Ecosystems strengthen as communities, founders, investors, and governments collaborate through catalytic platforms. And the narrative shifts as society begins to see wealth as responsibility rather than reward.

These are not utopian transformations. They are already visible in early catalytic structures, including the workforce financing model Hector describes in the Foreword. They are also beginning to appear across the world in climate funds, water portfolios, blue-carbon vehicles, community resilience bonds, digital health platforms, and regenerative agriculture models.

The catalytic future is not a fantasy. It is a trajectory waiting for ignition.

5. What the World Feels Like in The Possible Future

If catalytic philanthropy scales, the world in 2045 feels less brittle, less reactive, less unequal, less extractive, less anxious, less polarised. It feels more resilient, more regenerative, more interconnected, more dignified, more imaginative, more humane.

Catalytic capital cannot create this future alone. But without it, this future will remain out of reach.

6. Where This Leads

This chapter completes the arc of what catalytic capital can release if it becomes a global norm, and what happens if it does not. The final chapter is not structural or philosophical. It is personal. Because catalytic philanthropy is not ultimately about capital. It is about leadership.

The next chapter is the invitation. The moment when readers step into their own catalytic role.

CHAPTER EIGHT
THE INVITATION

Stepping Into The Possible Future

Every journey reaches a moment when understanding is no longer enough. A moment when analysis must become action. When possibility demands participation. When the future ceases to be something we predict and becomes something we shape.

This is that moment.

The Possible Future, a world where catalytic capital multiplies possibility, strengthens systems, and returns wealth to the world with coherence and courage, is not a theory. In practical terms, it means placing capital where uncertainty is highest so that other investors can participate once the risk is reduced.

It is a doorway. The only question is whether we choose to walk through it.

1. The Choice That Makes All the Difference

We often think the world changes because of big numbers, bold policies, or groundbreaking innovations. But systems shift because someone takes the first step, a step that alters the psychology of risk, the behaviour of institutions, and the momentum of capital. Catalytic capital is the manifestation of that step.

The invitation of this book is simple: move from generosity to activation, from impact to amplification, from accumulation to stewardship, from waiting to leading.

Catalytic philanthropy is not a larger form of giving. It is a different purpose for wealth. The decision to play a catalytic role, even at a small scale, can have disproportionate consequences. Systems move when someone chooses to go first.

That someone can be you.

2. The Personal Nature of Catalytic Leadership

Catalytic philanthropy is not fundamentally institutional. It is personal. Institutions do not take risks; people do. Boards do not feel urgency; individuals do. Family offices do not experience meaning; stewards do. Governments do not imagine new futures; leaders do.

Behind every catalytic moment in history, every first-loss tranche, every blended fund, every early anchor, every system-level shift, there is a person making a decision others were not yet ready to make. Hector Mujica's decision to design the Google Career Certificates Fund, described in the Foreword, is one such moment, when going first created the conditions for others to follow.

What it took was a person who understood that uncertainty is not the enemy, that risk has purpose, that timing shapes impact, that wealth carries responsibility, that leadership is relational, and that courage is contagious.

Catalytic leadership is not about heroism. It is about the willingness to see further, and then act accordingly.

3. What It Takes to Be Catalytic

Catalytic leadership requires three commitments.

The commitment to go first. Catalytic philanthropy begins before others are ready. It asks what becomes possible if we act now, who will follow once the perception of risk shifts, what system opens if we take the early step, what downstream capital is waiting for upstream courage. Going first is not recklessness. It is strategic initiation, the act that activates the sequence.

The commitment to design, not just give. Catalytic action is not about writing a larger cheque. It is about writing a different kind of cheque. It asks what role we are playing in the capital stack, what risk we are willing to absorb, what conditions should trigger capital release, what adjacent actors must be aligned, what systems must be supported. Catalytic capital is architected, not allocated. It requires thoughtfulness, clarity, and discipline.

The commitment to steward long time. Systems do not transform overnight. Catalytic capital requires the patience of ecosystems rather than the impatience of quarterly cycles. It asks what this will make possible in five years, how it will strengthen communities in ten, how the decision will ripple into the world our grandchildren inherit. The Possible Future is built by those who think in long time.

4. The Institutional Role: What Boards and Family Offices Must Do

While catalytic leadership is personal, catalytic infrastructure must be institutional. Boards, trustees, and investment committees must adopt catalytic investment policies, allocate pools of flexible capital, embed catalytic roles into governance, anchor early positions in blended vehicles, fund ecosystem work alongside direct services, measure amplification rather than only deployment, partner with government and private capital intentionally, and protect catalytic intent from mission drift.

Institutions shape the environment in which catalytic leaders act. Without institutional alignment, catalytic moments remain isolated ingenuity. With alignment, catalytic practice becomes a movement.

5. The Cultural Shift: What Wealth Must Become

Catalytic philanthropy is not merely an investment strategy. It represents a new story about wealth, what it is for, how it should move, and what it must serve. This new story recognises that wealth is not merely a marker of success but a resource for possibility, that it is not what you have but what you activate, that it must return to the world that enabled it, that it can be a force for regeneration rather than extraction, and that it is most meaningful when it multiplies opportunity for others.

This is the evolution of wealth consciousness emerging across generations. The next twenty years will redefine what it means to steward capital. Catalytic philanthropy is the expression of that redefinition.

6. The Collective Dimension: What Systems Need

Catalytic philanthropy does not operate in isolation. It works only when connected to a larger ecosystem. Systems require government partners willing to amplify proven models, private investors willing to follow catalytic signals, development finance institutions willing to share risk, corporations willing to join strategic coalitions, communities empowered to lead design, founders supported through early uncertainty, data systems that track amplification, and policy frameworks that institutionalise success.

Catalytic philanthropy becomes the connective tissue. It links these actors into coherence. The invitation is not simply to act. It is to coordinate.

7. What Happens When Catalytic Leadership Appears

When catalytic actors step into their role, three things happen.

Confidence shifts. Other capital follows. Government aligns. Markets respond. Communities gain stability. The psychological barrier dissolves.

Systems mobilise. Infrastructure strengthens. Solutions scale. Institutional actors coordinate. Ecosystems grow around catalytic anchors. The structural barrier dissolves.

Possibility expands. New markets emerge. Models replicate. Communities lead. Long-term resilience grows. Wealth gains coherence.

These transformations do not require perfect strategy. They require catalytic intent and catalytic timing.

8. The Responsibility and the Gift

Wealth carries two simultaneous truths. It is a responsibility, because wealth can either reinforce inequity or repair it. It is a gift, because wealth deployed with intention can accelerate solutions that would otherwise take decades to emerge.

Catalytic philanthropy unites both truths. It treats wealth not as a shield, but as a tool. Not as insulation, but as activation. The invitation is not to feel burdened. It is to feel empowered.

Catalytic capital gives people the ability to influence systems, reduce suffering, accelerate justice, strengthen communities, stabilise climate, restore ecosystems, and shape the trajectory of the world. This is not a small responsibility. It is not a small gift.

9. The Threshold We Now Stand On

We are living in decisive decades. The next twenty years will determine the trajectory of climate stability, food systems, mental health, education, democratic resilience, and community wellbeing. They will also determine the meaning of wealth for the next century.

On one path, wealth remains cautious, fragmented, and passive, stabilising old systems rather than activating new ones. On another path, wealth becomes catalytic, moving with purpose, absorbing early uncertainty, and multiplying hope at a scale not seen before.

The question is not which path is easier. The question is which path is worthy of this moment.

10. The Invitation

The invitation is simple. Step into the catalytic role only you can play.

Not because the world demands perfection, but because the world needs movement. Not because you must solve everything, but because your early act may release everything else. Not because you must transform the system alone, but because systems transform when the first move is made. Not because you are obligated, but because you are capable.

The Possible Future begins the moment you choose to act.

This is your invitation. Your moment. Your catalytic role. Your threshold into The Possible Future.

Everything that follows, the scaling, the alignment, the systems work, the community leadership, the global movement, begins when someone chooses to step first.

Let that someone be you.

EPILOGUE
THE POSSIBLE FUTURE, IN PRACTICE

The Possible Future is not an abstraction. It is a living movement shaped by the choices we make: the choices philanthropists make, the choices investors make, the choices governments make, the choices communities make, and the choices we make with our own imagination and courage.

All transformation begins quietly. It starts with people who recognise that the world is not only what it is, but what it could be.

This book has mapped the structural and philosophical architecture of catalytic capital. It has examined the Great Capital Return, the bottlenecks that keep wealth from moving, the multipliers that accelerate systems, the global signals already emerging, the values beneath the system, and the horizon twenty years ahead.

But architecture alone does not build the world. People do.

Catalytic philanthropy lives not in theory but in practice: in the specific acts of courage that allow others to follow, in the design choices that shift entire ecosystems, in the partnerships that bring public, private, and community capital into coherence.

The Possible Future begins when capital stops acting alone and begins acting as an amplifier. It begins when wealth stops orbiting itself and returns to the world with intention. It begins when leaders choose to move before the system is ready, because they understand the system will never be ready until someone chooses to move.

Transformation Through Action

If the world becomes more resilient over the next twenty years, if climate adaptation accelerates, if food and water systems regenerate, if health and mental health infrastructure expand, if education evolves, if communities stabilise, if institutions regain trust, it will not be because we discovered new technology, opened new markets, or passed new legislation.

It will be because capital flowed differently. Because catalytic philanthropists chose to go first. Because governments aligned their confidence with credible signals. Because private investors followed systems rather than speculation. Because communities were invited into leadership rather than left at the margins.

The Possible Future is not powered by money alone. It is powered by alignment, the point where wealth, wisdom, intention, and design meet.

What Remains After the Book Ends

Books can introduce ideas. They cannot keep up with the speed of the world. The catalytic field will continue to evolve, with new models, new structures, new failures, new breakthroughs, new institutions, and new movements.

That is why this book does not end with closure. It ends with continuation.

The Possible Future is a living conversation. It must remain alive, adaptive, iterative, real-time, and globally informed.

NOTES

The figures, sources, and reports cited in this book are drawn from the following:

Foreword

The Google Career Certificates Fund: launched 17 February 2022 by Google.org and Social Finance, with an initial commitment of USD 100 million. The program targets USD 1 billion in aggregate wage gains for more than 20,000 American learners over ten years, primarily through nonprofit training providers including Merit America and Year Up. Independent evaluation is being conducted by MDRC. Source: socialfinance.org and Google.org public announcements.

Prologue and Chapter One

US wealth transfer projection of USD 124 trillion by 2048, including USD 18 trillion to philanthropy: Cerulli Associates, *The Cerulli Report on U.S. High-Net-Worth and Ultra-High-Net-Worth Markets 2024: The Great Wealth Transfer*, December 2024.

Inequality figures (1 percent of population captured 41 percent of new wealth, bottom half captured 1 percent, between 2000 and 2024): G20 Extraordinary Committee of Independent Experts on Global Inequality, chaired by Joseph Stiglitz, presented to South African President Cyril Ramaphosa, November 2025. Drawing on data from the World Inequality Lab.

Foundation assets (USD 1.5 trillion globally, 90 percent of foundations under USD 10 million): Harvard Kennedy School Hauser Institute for Civil Society, *Global Philanthropy Report*, lead author Paula D. Johnson,

April 2018. Contemporary US foundation assets figure (close to USD 1.5 trillion): FoundationMark, reported via *Inside Philanthropy*, January 2024. Annual US foundation giving 2024 (USD 109 billion): *Giving USA 2025* and National Philanthropic Trust statistics.

Chapter Two

Global Philanthropy Environment Index figures (overall score 3.60, cross-border score 3.40): Indiana University Lilly Family School of Philanthropy, *Global Philanthropy Environment Index 2025*, released 28 May 2025.

Impact investing data (75 percent target market-rate returns; 6 percent of blended finance commitments from impact investors; 80 percent of those on commercial terms; 65 percent of concessional capital from public sources): Leah Pedersen, "Impact investing needs to rediscover its catalytic edge," *ImpactAlpha*, 8 October 2025. Underlying data drawn from GIIN *2024 Annual Impact Investor Survey* and Convergence *2025 State of Blended Finance*.

Chapters Three through Eight

Case studies in Chapters Three and Four are presented as composites drawing together documented patterns observed across catalytic finance practice, in line with the note at the front of this book. The Google Career Certificates Fund, referenced throughout via the Foreword, is the named, sourced anchor case.

Catalytic finance instruments and structures referenced throughout these chapters are drawn from the working practice of the field, including Convergence's database of blended finance transactions, the Catalytic Capital Consortium, and case material developed through MAD Ventures and partner institutions.

For a current and continually updated record of named ventures, structures, and case studies, see www.mad.vc/philanthropy

PROOF IN PRACTICE

A Living Library of Catalytic Capital

This movement deserves a home that evolves as the world evolves.

To honour the pioneers shaping catalytic capital, to share new models, to document what works and what fails, to showcase the systems already moving, and to surface lessons before they are lost, we have created a living library. It includes catalytic capital stacks, blended finance blueprints, and case studies from climate, water, food, health, and education. It documents global examples of philanthropy and government alignment, catalytic failures and what they teach, founder and community reflections, interviews with catalytic philanthropists, board members, and policy leaders, evolving definitions and frameworks, new research from global institutions, and updates as the field matures.

This library is continually updated. It serves as a companion to the book, a resource for practitioners, a blueprint for leaders, and a historical record of The Possible Future emerging in real time.

To explore the growing collection, visit **www.mad.vc/philanthropy**.

Returning to the Beginning

The question at the heart of this book remains: what becomes possible when wealth returns to the world that enabled it?

If catalytic philanthropy becomes a global practice, the answer is simple. Almost anything.

The Possible Future is not a promise. It is an invitation. An invitation to act with courage, to design with clarity, to steward with humility, to fund with imagination, and to return wealth to the world with coherence and purpose.

It begins with a signal. A decision. A first step.

It begins with the first dollar that chooses to move.

It begins with you.

ABOUT THE AUTHOR

Mark Falzon is a serial entrepreneur, investor, filmmaker, author, and global explorer with more than four decades of experience building, scaling, and reimagining ventures across multiple industries and continents. His career spans business, film, and finance, and his companies have placed four times in the BRW Fast 100, recognised among Australia's fastest-growing private companies. Throughout that journey, his work has consistently sat at the intersection of capital, leadership, and regenerative enterprise.

He is the co-founder of MAD Ventures, a Sydney-based platform dedicated to helping entrepreneurs, investors, and organisations build ventures that create meaningful economic, social, and environmental impact. Through MAD Ventures, Mark works with founders, family offices, and institutional investors to design strategies that align capital with long-term value creation across multiple industries and stages of growth.

His professional focus is the architecture of capital systems: how capital moves, where it stalls, and what structural choices determine whether ventures succeed or fail. He has spent more than two decades working alongside business leaders through periods of transition, expansion, succession, and exit. That work has shaped his belief that catalytic capital, capital placed early, with patience and intent, is one of the most underused tools available to those who steward wealth.

Mark is the co-creator of the Venture Compass, an integrated framework combining business strategy, investment design, and human leadership development. He is the creator of Métis, a leadership and decision-making framework drawing on classical wisdom traditions and modern systems thinking. He is also the co-creator of Solyrais and Synarchos, profiling tools designed to strengthen alignment between life partners and between co-founders. These frameworks are applied across his investment activities, his work with founders, and the books he writes.

Beyond MAD Ventures, Mark mentors a small number of founders and CEOs each year through Behind The Scenes, his private mentoring practice, and convenes peer communities of investors and entrepreneurs working at the leading edge of catalytic and impact-aligned capital. His perspective is shaped not only by business and finance but also by his work as a filmmaker and global explorer, experiences that have informed his interest in the human, cultural, and systemic dimensions of how value is created and shared.

He is the author of five books, including MAD: What the World Needs Now Is a Little Madness, which explores the role of entrepreneurship and courageous leadership in building businesses that matter. Several further books are in development, examining the relationship between capital, character, and the institutions that shape our shared future.

Through his writing, advisory work, and investment activities, he continues to explore how capital can move from accumulation toward activation, and how catalytic leadership can release the systems required for the next century.

Learn more at: www.markfalzon.com

Made in United States
Troutdale, OR
11/03/2026

56844634R00050